Victorian Houses

A TREASURY OF
LESSER-KNOWN EXAMPLES

FRONTISPIECE. Lenox, Mass. (Photo by H.H. Sidman, *The American Architect,* 5 April 1902). The W.D. Sloane house, Elm Court, had just acquired an addition when this picture was taken at the beginning of the present century. Peabody and Stearns, of Boston, were the architects. The old shingled building in the H. H. Richardson style was sheer simplicity compared to the elaborate white limestone and stained timberwork of the new section. Such archaeological intricacies as it showed soon were to stifle and eventually snuff out Victorian eclecticism. Queen Victoria died about the time the photograph was taken and before it was published: the Victorian era officially had ended.

Victorian Houses

A TREASURY OF
LESSER-KNOWN EXAMPLES

Edmund V. Gillon, Jr.
AND
Clay Lancaster

DOVER PUBLICATIONS, INC., NEW YORK

Published in Canada by General Publishing
Company, Ltd., 30 Lesmill Road, Don Mills,
Toronto, Ontario.
Published in the United Kingdom by Constable
and Company, Ltd., 10 Orange Street, London,
WC 2.

*Victorian Houses: A Treasury of Lesser-Known
Examples* is a new work, first published in 1973
by Dover Publications, Inc. The photographs are
by Mr. Gillon, except where otherwise noted in
Mr. Lancaster's introduction and captions.

International Standard Book Number: 0-486-22966-1
Library of Congress Catalog Card Number: 73-77197

Manufactured in the United States of America
Dover Publications, Inc.
31 East 2nd Street
Mineola, N.Y. 11501

INTRODUCTION

The architectural monstrosities of the Victorian period have been created by twentieth-century ignorance. Ignorance, the root of religious bigotry, racial prejudice, dread of divergent social systems, and repulsion to unfamiliar forms in music, drama, art and architecture, is a deficiency in the perceiver, not in the thing perceived. Modern people, subscribing to the organic principle in building (whereby outer forms follow inner function), naturally would lack understanding of the Victorian practice of arranging rooms in masses built for pictorial effect. One is centrifugal, the other centripetal. The traditional theory in Western culture is that architecture is style (whether Classic orders, Gothic arches and tracery, or exotic finery) applied to structure. The Victorians brought the concept to its logical conclusion. Theirs was a world rich in the accumulated motifs of past civilizations, from which they borrowed copiously, and — it must not be overlooked — to which they added creatively. They were so successful in the lushness of their results, that the modern period could add nothing and had to react against them in order to retain its integrity. Contemporary critics accuse the Victorians of needless complexity, of extraneous clutter. But is this not a frank admission of the twentieth-century failure to comprehend the nineteenth-century attraction to design articulation? Theirs was an architectural vocabulary full of meanings to which our eyes and ears have become insensitive, and of which our minds have become ignorant.

Our culture pales through comparison to the colorful domain of the Victorians. Heirs and beneficiaries of the Medieval, Georgian and Classic modes, and the beginning of the Revivals (in America only a little less so than in Britain), the English-speaking world of the 1800s launched an eclecticism equal to and surpassing that of the Imperial Period of ancient Rome. It was outgoing, consistent with the contemporary progress of empire expansion of both Great Britain and the United States. Pre-Victorian English pride over holdings in South Asia had been expressed in the Indian Mughal-style remodeling and enlarging of the Palace at Brighton in 1818-21; and American vanity in its intercourse with China (forbidden prior to the Revolution) was manifested in the Pagoda and Labyrinth Garden built at the foremost seaport of Philadelphia in 1827. Other examples might be cited dating from before Victoria's coronation as Queen of England and Ireland in 1837. Shortly thereafter, the British constructed the mammoth Houses of Parliament (1840-60), on the Thames, in the indigenous Gothic manner. For some time before and during this era, the national style in the United States was Greek Revival, in large measure due to the principle of liberty that was symbolized by the ancient city-states of the Aegean. But there was too much ferment in the industrializing nations of the nineteenth century for them to be content with a limited range of inspiration. They were prompted to draw deeply from history, nature, geometry, theory, and from their own innate capacity for invention. The resulting Eclecticism veered into as many channels as architects and designers working at it. Another consideration is that whereas earlier empires reflected the great breadth of their domains in official edifices in the capital, nineteenth-century democracy filtered free expression down to smaller proletariat cottages in the hinterlands. The phenomenon seems overwhelming, until one learns to expect it everywhere and recognizes the streams that nurtured it.

There are two levels of Victorian architecture. The upper is the sophisticated, urban province of trained, name artist-architects. The lower is the somewhat naive, provincial realm of unschooled, anonymous carpenter-builders. The works of the first group are more easily analyzed by those familiar with architectural history, whence their elements were derived. Those of the second can be deduced from an acquaintance with the first; but not in every instance, as sometimes motifs borrowed or badly remembered have become so altered as to defy identity. What is lost in authenticity is more than made up for in quaintness and uniqueness. Though the British may look upon all of American architecture as provincial, such is not the case. In this collection of lesser-known Victorian houses along the East Coast are examples showing a high degree of sophistication; and the range extends down to some of utmost innocence. The extremes are exemplified by the great masonry Samuel Colt villa at Hartford, Connecticut (Plates 60-61), and the little vertical-board cottage in Montpelier, Vermont (Plates 12-13). The former combines bracketed, arched and domed forms from the Mediterranean and Middle East, and the latter uses the simple structural system set forth in *Upjohn's Rural Architecture* (1852), with an oversized leaf cutout sprouting from vergeboards and over openings, plus a few incidental trefoil details. The two buildings — so different in scale, materials, setting and effect — are alike in recognizing the need for extraneous ornament to enliven and clothe the anatomy of the building. Each is handled according to the scope and taste of the architect or builder. Other examples in this *Treasury* interlay (some nearly equal to one or the other of) these ultimates.

The more than one hundred buildings pictured are from the upper Eastern Seaboard. Almost three-fourths of them are located in New England, one-fourth in the Middle States of New York, New Jersey and Pennsylvania, and a few farther south and some in Canada. As suggested by the subtitle, the intention of this album has not been to present the best-known examples, or, for that matter, the best, architecturally considered. The selection was made somewhat arbitrarily as they were encountered during the peregrinations of Edmund Gillon, who unquestionably has a good eye for an authentic example and interesting picture subject. This would be a unique method for an architectural survey or study: but this book is not either of them. In two words the main title states a period and a type of building. The period is the last three-quarters of the nineteenth century; the type is the detached dwelling, with a few examples of the duplex. The great majority of houses shown are "anonymous," meaning built by and for people who were never heard of outside their own time and community, and soon forgotten locally. The collection purports to supplement other published works that are "architectural heritage" or "homes of the great" in nature. It is most important, in recording a civilization, that the "everyday" art, and buildings, be included. This *Treasury* fills the gap in its special field.

A standardizing factor in home building throughout the United States during the mid to end of the nineteenth century was the house-pattern book. The most prominent and influential were the volumes of Andrew Jackson Downing, especially *Cottage Residences* (1842) and *The Architecture of Country Houses* (1850), in which were models for the cottages shown in Plates 22 and 23 and houses in Plates 9, 10 and 24. The dwelling in Plate 30 was designed by Calvert Vaux and published as Design 14 in the architect's *Villas and Cottages* (1857). Orson Squire Fowler's *A Home for All* (1848) inaugurated a vogue for octagons, to which the subject of Plate 14 is beholden. The Italian Renaissance house in Plate 41 is linked with a Downing quotation, but its details may have been inspired by designs in Thomas U. Walter's *Two Hundred Designs for Cottages and Villas* (1846). The bracketed villas in Plates 40 and 46–47 may have been patterned after Samuel Sloan plans published in *The Model Architect* (1852). The towered clapboard mansard of Plate 50 is a restrained version of a Gilbert Bostwick Croff scheme from *Progressive American Architecture* (1875). Plate 89 is reprinted from William M. Woolett's *Old Homes Made New* (1878). The "Queen Anne" house in Lowell (Plate 96) is of the type depicted so often in the *American Architect and Building News* and *The New York Sketch Book,* two periodicals that began publication during the mid 1870s. The Cape May "Stick Style" house (Plate 98) reflects features from illustrations in *Palliser's New Cottage Homes* (1887); and the little East Longmeadow cottage (Plate 2) has points in common with sketches in Carl Pfeiffer's *American Mansions and Cottages* (1889).

In all probability most Yankee Victorian builders had a limited acquaintance with architectural pattern books and magazines. They were better aware of what was being constructed, at least locally, and their vista ranged outwardly mostly as far as they, or their clients, had traveled. Also, talk of buildings going up in the cultural centers of Paris, London and New York had greater reverberation than mute authors' dream houses. Thus Visconti and Lefuel's Nouveau Louvre (1850-51), in the Mansard manner, Gilbert Scott's St. Pancras Hotel (1867), in Venetian Gothic, and the Buckingham (1876, at Fifth Avenue and 50th Street, New York), in Reconstruction-period Eclecticism, may have set the pattern for more middle-class American residences of the last quarter of the nineteenth century than designs from books. As a matter of count, almost one-third of the examples shown in this album are Mansard insofar as the roof form is concerned. Half as many are Victorian Gothic, and an equal number are eclectic. The next most numerous category is the bracketed style, a convergence from all those regions in which deep overhanging eaves abound, including Italy, Spain, the Alps, the Near East and southern India. Individualized from this group are Italian villas, Swiss chalets, and American farmhouse types — the last as defined by Downing in describing Plate XVII in *Country Houses.* Early to mid-Victorian structures are comparatively forthright in style persuasion, whereas those postdating the Civil War become involved and complicated. They are Eclectic, borrowing motifs and combining them without restriction, and devising and adding original forms as they seem appropriate. The desired end was visual effect, mostly considered from the outside. The early phase was that of the simple Revivals — Classic, Greek, Gothic, Romanesque and Renaissance — and the later was that appropriately called Picturesque Eclecticism.

Special attention should be directed toward two aspects of late nineteenth-century American architecture, as being outstanding and meaningful in the maze of Picturesque Eclecticism. Both were imported to the States from England. One is the Eastlake manner, named after Charles Locke Eastlake, author of *History of the Gothic Revival* (1872), the first book on the subject, and *Hints on Household Taste* (1868), republished in the United States in seven editions from 1872 to 1883. The Eastlake manner is characterized by details of stylized, flat, linear floral designs, that are like jigsaw work in wood, shallow incised patterns in brownstone, and silhouettes in delicate iron crestings (Plates 51, 74 and 75). They are somewhat Oriental (arabesque and Japanese) in quality. The other type is the "Queen Anne," which term has been mentioned earlier, a more generalized architectural style that may include Eastlake ornaments. The designation recalls the period in England at the beginning of the eighteenth century (during the reign of the daughter of James II), when it was the practice to mix Gothic and Renaissance elements, sometimes in the most promiscuous fashion. The chief protagonist of the Victorian-era "Queen Anne" in Britain was Richard Norman Shaw, who worked from the late 1860s onward. His counterparts in America performed during the late 1870s through the 1890s. The hallmark was a protruding bay window with rounded sides and featuring a Palladian window on the front plane, as in Shaw's New Zealand

Chambers (1872) in London. Compound forms, tall and multiple-shafted chimneys, assorted gables, projecting and receding porches, a mixture of materials (stone, brick, slate, terracotta, wood and stucco), and lavish details typify the "Queen Anne" style (Plates 96, 105, 106, 110 and 111). Combined with the Alpine chalet form, "Queen Anne" became the American Stick Style (Plates 98, 99, 101 and 108).

The "Queen Anne" occasionally absorbed early Georgian elements in the United States and became the Colonial Revival, whose examples sometimes showed strong relationship to the original models (Plate 109) and sometimes very little (Plate 100). The Colonial Revival survived most of the other types of Victorian architecture, flourishing up to World War I, and it was given some patronage afterward. Its longevity may be attributed to its having latched onto and aroused sentiment over the early historic types in the New World. In this the Colonial Revival departed somewhat from the important creative eclectic interest of Victorianism proper. It should be mentioned, as well, that Art Nouveau constituted another tangent whose secession tendencies excluded it from the main orbit of Victorian rotation. Art Nouveau stressed originality to the extent of eliminating eclectic borrowing. The United States saw next to nothing of Art Nouveau architecture such as was manifested in Europe, but it had its own special brand in the American bungalow. The American bungalow is the exact antithesis of traditional Western architecture, to which all loyal branches of Picturesque Eclecticism adhered. Bungalow design eschewed the panoply of architectonic forms applied to the vertical wall; it even subjugated the vertical wall, pulling it in under the all-important bungalow roof, casting it in the shade, literally, under its deep, overhanging eaves. Although it got started in this country around 1880, the real era of the bungalow here was the first quarter of the nineteenth century, which postdates the Victorian time span and thus is not included in the present collection.

The primary purpose of this book is to foster enjoyment of nineteenth-century domestic structures through the visual record. In the introduction the attempt has been made to present an overall vista of the subject, to better fit into place the individual examples shown. Comments beneath the pictures make reference to sources of inspiration, find comparisons with other examples presented, point out special design features, sometimes remark on changes and alterations, and, in the case of photographs contemporary with the subject, give the name of the resident builder.

Extant Victorian buildings are becoming progressively fewer. With private enterprise, and Urban Renewal and other official agents currently bent on destroying America's architectural heritage, it is fortunate that Mr. Gillon has found and photographed so many houses in quasi-pristine condition. He has supplemented his own shots with copies from late nineteenth- and early twentieth-century picture books, including the "Illustrated" series *(Leominster, Lowell* and *Hartford,* 1899), the "Sunlight Pictures" series *(Amherst,* 1891, and *Hartford,* 1892), and regional surveys, such as M. F. Sweetser's *Picturesque Maine* (1880), C. L. Howe's *Views of Charleston, New Hampshire,* and two surveys of Woburn and Lee, Massachusetts. One can spot the old views, as they are without telephone and utility wires, television aerials, automobiles and other technological disfigure-

ments of recent times. If this were all that our times have inflicted upon the Victorian landmark, we could consider ourselves fortunate. Modern grossness has gone further and obliterated the original autumnal paint colors (whereby the house merged visually into its environment), substituting unimaginative white, reproducing the tone and effect of bleached dry bones. Of the two prevalent present-day uses for such buildings, that of guest house is less appropriate than the alternative of funeral home. The true architectural monstrosities of the Victorian period are those that have been created by twentieth-century perversion of taste, which is a form of ignorance.

Nantucket   CLAY LANCASTER
December, 1972

Original form of the Brinkerhoff House in Poughkeepsie (see PLATE 48).

PLATE 1.   Cambridge, N. Y. If any single house type can be called typical of the Hudson River Valley at the beginning of the latter half of the nineteenth century, it would be the small two-story square box form, with near-flat roof extended as overhanging eaves on fancy coupled brackets. A parlor and hall in breadth across the front, the facade is three-bayed; and such scheme is common to the row house in the city and to farm house alike. The detached variety, however, has windows at the sides, a front porch, and, if view warranted it, a cupola as crowning device. The flagpole proclaims its Americanism, though devoid of the star-spangled banner itself. The national colors are here: red house, white snow and blue sky.

PLATE 2.   East Longmeadow, Mass. Vertical boards with weatherstripping at the top and horizontal clapboards below constitute the wall covering of this little house, that is asymmetrical above and more or less balanced in the first story. The porch is made up of pieces of wood fitted together and referred to as the "Stick Style." Something of the same manner of joining pieces char- acterizes the window frames. The oversized window in the dormer and under- sized fenestration on the same level to the right are to be expected in the period. Bargeboards and finials of the gables are or have jigsaw cutouts. The lattices in the apex triangles are characteristically Chinese, which Far Eastern motifs make it a counterpart to the example opposite.

PLATE 3.   Millbury, Mass. Two generations younger yet still bearing a family resemblance to the temple-type Greek Revival cottage ancestor of the 1820s, this dwelling reflects the changes that have beset architecture during the interim. Distortion of members is manifested in the substitution of light bracketed lattice piers for heavy pillars; and the triangular pediment has been thrust upward, its tympanum pierced by a Japanese writing-alcove or tea-house bell-shaped opening. It creates an upper recessed porch, where the family gathered together — Rogers group fashion — replace the marble sculptures of scantily draped gods and goddesses in the Greek pediment archetype.

PLATE 4.   Medway, Mass. Greek Revival, virtually the national style in the United States from about 1820 to the outbreak of the Civil War, was bold, masculine and simple. Late examples often became ornamented, combining several orders (here Ionic and Tower-of-the-Winds Corinthian), using fenes-tration variety, including bay windows and wreaths around circular garret openings, and a crowning cupola. The cupola here is hexagonal and has voluted capitals to the stubby supports at the corners.

PLATE 5.   Thomaston, Me. The specimen above has gone a step further than the foregoing, combining bracketed elements with Greek Revival. The result is a strange conglomeration. Very unarchitectonic, the extremities of the shallow porch rest upon shuttered bay windows, with a pair of slender Ionic columns flanking the doorway. The cast-iron lyre motif in the upper railing is more Rococo than Classic. The banister with pedestal posts across the front of the platform accords with nothing else.

PLATE 6. Port Clyde, Me. A late eighteenth-century type of twin-chimney residence with advanced entrance pavilion crowned by a gable, the house retains such original classic details as "eared" enframements and cornice hoods over the typical six-paned, double-sash windows, modillions in the gable, and quoins at the upright extremities. Victorian alterations have changed the doorway and chimneys, and added a bracketed side porch and sunken cupola in the roof ridge, and perhaps the dormers. Despite these modifications the building retains a Georgian design quietude that sets it apart from wholly Victorian houses.

PLATE 7.   Concord, N. H. The pedimented center pavilion, featured on the last two examples and this one, here is a portico showing the complete disintegration of the Greek Revival style. It has not only brackets supporting the deep cornice but a sort of steamboat-gothic spandrel beneath the architrave of the portico. Coupled windows with drip hood molds are other decadent Greek characteristics. The balconies accord with the steamboat element. Note the Gothic pointed window or upper doorway that opens on the center balcony.

PLATE 8.   Rural Conn. Hand-me-down clothes are suggested by the ill-fitting dress of this old farmhouse. In remodeling, front and rear walls have been heightened to accommodate the gaudy paired brackets, so that the gables no longer span the flanks of the house but end in horizontal shelves. On the near side of the main block a bay window has been squeezed between the wing porch and front corner of the house. The squat pillars of the entrance portico have Tower-of-the-Winds capitals, that would be correctly proportioned on a column about the height of the entire facade.

PLATE 9.   Fitchburg, Mass. A. J. Downing's *The Architecture of Country Houses* (1850) presented numerous simple rectangular designs resembling this house. They were labeled "Suburban Cottage" and called "Bracketed" or "American" in style. Their porch or "veranda" was like the one pictured, and gables followed the same scheme. The Fitchburg house might be considered more American than the Downing designs, because of the pilasters at the corners and entablature part way across the front in the Greek Revival manner. Downing eschewed the "national" style in favor of more picturesque modes.

PLATE 10. Rural area around Woodstock, Vt. This and the example opposite, and three others farther along (Plates 28, 29 and 103) are houses in the Swiss chalet style. The type was introduced to America through Designs X and XIV in Downing's *Country Houses,* the book mentioned under the previous plate. Each of the chalets is located in a different state, and each is of a slightly different type. The one shown above holds to the most conservative American small-house plan, with center doorway, windows symmetrically placed, and a chimney in the middle. The deeply overhanging eaves and balcony spanning the front constitute its chalet characteristics.

PLATE 11.   Farmington, Me. A prosaic duplex house achieves distinction through combining crude natural porch posts with slender banisters and graceful cutouts suspended from the bargeboards. In all likelihood these features were suggested by the Downing description of the ideal chalet. It is "rude in construction, and rustic and quaint in ornaments and details" *(Country Houses,* 1850, p. 123). Be that as it may, the decoration does not alter the simple, bilateral balance, which is not the proper shape for a picturesque Alpine house.

PLATES 12-13. Montpelier, Vt. Upright boards with external insulation strips had a widespread vogue in America after publication of Richard Upjohn's *Rural Architecture* in 1852. Though designs in it were predominantly for country churches, the surface treatment was used on all kinds of buildings, usually of unpretentious nature. It figures on this Montpelier cottage and its dependency. A bit of refinement appears in the grape-leaf frieze and open

Gothic tracery over the projecting entrance vestibule, and the fenestration has lozenge panes, with one small window being of lozenge shape. The striking and unifying motif is the lobated leaf cutout that forms hoods over the openings, making tall rectangles look arched. Pendant from the rakings, it contributes considerable character to the gables.

PLATE 14. Farmington, Me. Dwellings of regular polygonal form were propagated by Orson Squire Fowler, a phrenologist of Fishkill, New York, through his volume, *A Home for All,* subtitled, *The Octagon Mode of Building,* published in 1848. The Farmington house departs from the protagonist's ideals: it was built of brick instead of poured concrete (capable of assuming odd angles); it has buttresses at the corners and curious brickwork projections under the eaves (neither functional nor necessary); and it lacks the prescribed encompassing verandahs (for relaxing, or exercising during inclement weather), though it seems once to have had an entrance porch. The cupola at the apex of the low-pitched roof lights the staircase that is the circulation core of the house.

PLATE 15.   Ipswich, Mass. Related to the regular geometric house plan is this square residence on South Village Green in Ipswich. It is thought that the building was built in the 1830s by a man named Baker; and if so, one is at a loss to account for the four identical facades. It was owned after 1852 by Augustine Heard, and one suspects that he was bitten by the Fowler bug and gave the house its definitive and present form. Circumstantial evidence is contributed to the thesis by the octagonal cupola and the hanging staircase that occupies the center of the house.

PLATE 16. Lunenburg, Nova Scotia. A complicated effect has been achieved in a provincial Canadian cottage by frontal protuberances on a basically rectangular clapboard structure covered by a simple pitched roof. The reduplicated convex bonnets over the polygonal bay windows probably derived from mansard roofs, but they look somewhat like Chinese pagodas. Striving for a free and varied design has backfired into a tight clutter of naive elements.

PLATE 17. Barrington, Nova Scotia. Compared to the Lunenburg house of similar size opposite, here the rectangular projections accord with the house shape and seem integral; and the scale between parts is valid. Semicircular arches beneath triangular pediments in forms penetrating the roof and ogee blind arches on slender pilasters in the first story furnish motifs for the two levels. Otherwise there is a rectangular facade scheme that extends down to the panels in the base of the bay windows. Note the fish-scale imbrication in the gables.

PLATE 18. Granville Ferry, Nova Scotia. The late nineteenth-century penchant for bay windows in Nova Scotia accounts for discordant features in an otherwise charming and logical conception. The fenestration on the shallow porches is crowded, and the innermost lights stare at the walls of the projecting pavilion. No doubt the awkward pendant in the porch tracery came about through eliminating the middle post that obstructed the view. Inside, the staircase rises in front of the recess created by the center bay window and renders it inaccessible. Gothic cutout bargeboards and spire finials on the steeply pitched gables are redeeming elements.

PLATE 19. Cheticamp, Nova Scotia. The advanced center pavilion appears again on a rural Canadian cottage, only here it is surrounded by a porch. Supports are square posts capped by brackets, and stairs are at either end of the forward section. Plain raking boards on overhanging eaves frame the tall front gable, which is nearly filled by a double-arched window and oculus centered in the pointed head. Be it accident or design, changes in the roof planes create an unusually pleasing and forthright architectural mass.

PLATE 20. Shelburne, Nova Scotia. Basically the same sequence of elements used in the Barrington house (Plate 17), upper and lower motifs of different character are carried horizontally across the facade. Here they are more lacy. Protruding gables are superimposed on the rectangular bay windows and external entry as though an afterthought. Window heads in the second story are corbel arched out of necessity from the restricted spaces provided. Gothic tracery embellishes horizontal cornices, balcony railing and sloping vergeboards. Refined and delicately shaped are the pinnacles atop the gables.

PLATE 21. Granville Ferry, Nova Scotia. The five preceding examples will have combined into a simplified image of the typical Canadian provincial cottage: it is rectangular, with end gables, two insignificant chimneys on the roof ridge, and forms pushing forward sporting architectural finery. This sixth specimen conforms to the type, yet it surpasses the others in diversity of ornament and disregard for scale. Juxtaposed against a triple window of studio proportions is a minuscule balcony in the center bay, and heavy undulating festoons under the overhanging eaves contrast severely with the light and static details of the porch. Noteworthy also is the bold departure from bilateral symmetry in setting the longest bay of the verandah at one end.

PLATE 22.   Portland, Me. The Print Department of the Metropolitan Museum of Art owns a sheet bearing a perspective sketch and floor plans for an "English Cottage." The drawings are by Alexander Jackson Davis, New York architect, and are thought to have been sent to A. J. Downing during preparation of his *Cottage Residences*. They are reflected in engravings as Design II in the book published in 1842, in reverse, no doubt due to the plates being printed backwards. The form is quite similar to the cottage in Maine, although the porch has three sections, like that on the house opposite. The Davis-Downing building is meant to be built of brick, stuccoed to look like stone; whereas here the material is wood, rusticated for a stone effect.

PLATE 23. Thompson, Conn. Position of the chimneys indicates this cottage to have a plan more like that of Design II in *Cottage Residences* than the house opposite. Use of clapboards ignores the prescribed surface recommended. Windows have rectangular rather than diamond-shaped panes; and the walls are higher, with dormers added on the roof. Only slight differences appear in the porch: in the Downing design, spandrels over the central arch are like those in the Maine cottage (but not having pendants); as here, the center pinnacle is taller; and there are crenelations over the side bays, which may have existed and been removed from this house.

PLATE 24.   Cazenovia, N.Y. A less pretentious house than the two preceding examples, the type is Carpenter's Gothic. Walls are of vertical boards, as on the Montpelier cottage (Plates 12-13). The bargeboard motif here is simplified to lobes of identical size with trefoil bosses at their points. Tracery spandrels and railings of the porch are considerably abbreviated and diminished, although posts remain large. Diamond-paned windows and hood molds, the way the porch follows the plan outline of the facade, bay windows at the ends, and the lush verdant backdrop contribute to a satisfying impression.

PLATE 25. Geneva, N.Y. Although built of masonry, the house shown above better illustrates Carpenter's Gothic than the wood example opposite. Reference is made to the details, which of course are of wood. Raking boards are simple scallops, except for a loop at the base; and the rather constricted arches of the porch do not even have trefoils in the spandrels, though crenelations form a simple cresting. Gables graduate in size from right to left, the farthest stepping forward and wider in angle than the other two.

PLATE 26. South Robbinston, Me. The more cursive, flat vergeboards in these two examples (on this page and opposite), the rather un-Gothic patterns in the lattices between the coupled porch supports, and particularly the large projecting dormer windows in the one on this page indicate they both belong to a period later than those closer to the Downing models. The fragility of the porch and dip in its roof reminds us that Downing — like most of his contemporaries — believed that all architecture derived from the first human shelters of the cave and the tent. The exceedingly deep gable eaves further the tent-origin concept. A subtle refinement is curved muntins at the tops of first-story windows, forming pointed arches, like those made by branching stanchions and Gothic window heads in the second story.

PLATE 27. Northern Vt. The ultimate in Carpenter's Gothic consists of box-like forms covered by high-peaked roofs, and with trim more ornamental than architectural. Complexity of pavilions and wings does not alter the rule. The doll-house look is inevitable, with the scale between parts often awry. The little pavilion at the right-hand end resembles a commercial, child's gingerbread house, cardboard or pastry. All of the bargeboards are like swags hung from the gables for holiday decorations.

PLATE 28. Stoughton, Mass. The two examples shown on these pages come closer to the true chalet than those in Plates 10 and 11, having a full second story and low-pitched, bracketed roofs. However, in the one above the open timberwork is more decorative than structural, as in the Swiss pro-

totype. A. J. Downing declared (in *Country Houses,* 1850, p. 123) the species "especially adapted to . . . wild and romantic scenery," like that where they originated; but American versions usually are set in a flat landscape — often in a village.

PLATE 29. Tolland, Conn. Alpine characteristics are reflected in the deeply suspended balcony and eaves, ornamental woodwork, and the departure from the rigid rectangular plan. Inconsistent with the rusticity of the originals are the prim Victorian dressmaker-type scallops under the arches and balcony ledges, and other cutouts in the railings. The modern bleached color scheme and staccato planting reflect the same mentality.

PLATE 30.   Newburgh, N.Y. Calvert Vaux, a young English architect, came to the United States in 1850 to work with A. J. Downing; but their association was cut short by the drowning of the latter two years later. Vaux published his own book of plans for *Villas and Cottages* in 1857, made up in large measure from his own commissions. Design 14 is of that built for W. E. Warren in Downing's home town of Newburgh. Comparing the house today — pictured above — with the perspective sketch in the book reveals that it has remained unchanged (the front dormers seem an original afterthought) save for the addition of the spidery trellises to each side of the entrance. Vaux's buildings differ from Downing's in having slightly heavier architectural dress.

PLATE 31.   Woburn, Mass. (Board of Trade, *Woburn, An Historical and Descriptive Sketch of the Town,* Woburn, 1885). The Julius F. Ramsdell house on Glenwood Street relates to no specific Old World style. Critic A. J. Downing and Architect A. J. Davis would have characterized it as in the bracketed or American farmhouse manner, and they would have made the outer walls vertical boards. Calvert Vaux would have used clapboards, as here, with brick fill. The Ramsdell house resembles in form and plan Design 1 in *Villas and Cottages,* although the constructed house is larger and shows later features, such as larger window panes and square-piered instead of lattice supports to the porch. In the stone fence each block has dressed edges around bush-hammered raised areas.

PLATE 32. Belfast, Me. The similarities between this and the Warren house by Vaux in Newburgh (Plate 30) suggest a connection. It could have been that the residence in Maine derived from Design 14 in *Villas and Cottages,* or it could have come from another source. In the mid-nineteenth century, as today, periodicals carried ideas for prospective home owners. These were not strictly "home" magazines, but of the general, literary type; and thus they reached a more diversified audience. In the November 1855 issue of *Harpers New Monthly Magazine,* Calvert Vaux wrote an illustrated article, entitled "Hints for Country House Builders," in which appeared two sketches of the Warren house. In the three-quarter rear view the gable dip seems more pronounced, as on the Belfast dwelling.

PLATE 33.   Woodstock Hill, Conn. A rather large residence to make use of vertical boards and weatherstripping — certainly all of the main block and probably most of the ell are original. The principal mass is square, with center hallways transverse and crosswise, one projecting as a two-story pavilion at the front and the other as a canopied porte-cochère on the right flank. Cut-out wood crestings, like crenelations, enliven the cornices of the single-storied elements, including the traceried porches. The lower part of the entrance pavilion has curious splayed corners.

PLATE 34. Seneca Falls, N.Y. The decadence of the decorative elements indicate the late date of this cottage. Details are Gothic Revival. The drip molds over the first-story openings have shrunken to a minimum. Pierced spandrels in the porch meander without conviction. Jigsaw cutouts under the gable curl without direction. The dormers are wholly unrelated to everything else and must have been put in later without consideration for the existing design.

PLATE 35.   Fitchburg, Mass. The cutout bargeboard resembles that of the house opposite, only here it is more rhythmic and constitutes the only decorative element of an otherwise restrained design. Walks lead from the iron and stone fence to twin entrances. The walls are of horizontal flush boards; and the windows are framed by simple moldings and equipped with louvred shutters. Modern trellises tend to pull the eye away from the original and singular eaves ornamentation.

PLATE 36. Wellsville, N.Y. The medium-sized house on the Mediterranean may be traced back to the Etruscans, and it is the longest lived of any Western domestic type. Its details reflect something of the antique classic tradition. Its forms, resulting from additions, are irregular and picturesque. It was inevitable that the type would be adopted in the Romantic Period. England's first example was Cronkhill, designed by John Nash and built at Attingham in 1802. The first in the United States was the Bishop Doane house at Burlington, New Jersey, by John Notman and dating from 1837. An asymmetrical mass is dominated by a tower, usually with the entrance at its base. Ornament sources were limitless: in this version from the late 1860s, built for pharmacist Edwin Bradford Hall at Wellsville, inspiration seems to have derived from the interior decorator's stencils, lambrequins, fringe and tassels.

PLATE 37. New Castle, Del. The irregular massing of the Italian villa bears a stronger relation to that of the Gothic Revival than to any other contemporary style. The main difference between them is the roof pitch, which is higher in the northern, medieval style, for more readily shedding rain and holding up under snow. Token respect to the proper slope is shown in the roofs of the tower and principal pavilion of this American southern house, whereas subsidiary wings have a practically flat covering. The gable facing us is within a few degrees of the angle of the two on the Wellsville Italian-villa facade. Gothic affinities of the New Castle building tend rather to such details as pointed windows, hood molds, lobated vergeboards, pinnacles and chimney stacks.

PLATE 38. East Douglas, Mass. The plain square house with low-pitched hipped roof and deep bracketed eaves was called the Tuscan or Italianate villa in the middle of the nineteenth century. The first of its kind in the United States was built for John Cridland near Philadelphia, designed by the English-born architect, John Haviland. He later published its design in *The Builder's Assistant,* issued in three volumes in 1818, 1819 and 1821. Downing's Design VII in *Country Houses* followed the same lines and popularized the type. Its porch has affinities to that on the house pictured. The cupola was a later innovation.

PLATE 39.   Stonington, Conn. Windows with two lights, columns coupled in the portico, alternating large and small brackets and the break in the cornice line indicate a later date for this Italianate villa. The grossness of the column capitals, crudeness of the scalloped portico cresting, shallow main cornice projection, and disproportioned octagonal cupola testify to the decadence of the type only a short while after its flowering. The iron paling in the foreground was cast for balconies rather than for yard fences.

PLATE 40.   Cape May, N.J. The culmination of the Tuscan villa was a tall bracketed cube, in the manner of designs by Samuel Sloan of Philadelphia, such as were illustrated in his two-volume plan book, *The Model Architect* (1852). Philadelphians summering on the New Jersey coast transplanted it to the cape island. In this specimen the third-story fenestration is organized in a frieze or attic, shared with the ubiquitous brackets. The cupola is reminiscent of a ship's pilothouse. The sign in the entrance bay attests to the commodiousness of the house, offering a choice of "APARTMENTS — ROOMS."

PLATE 41.   New Haven, Conn. A. J. Downing's *Landscape Gardening,* 1841, presents the sketch of a squarish house resembling the one above, captioned, "The New Haven Suburban Villa." A footnote explains: "New Haven abounds with tasteful residences. 'Hillhouse Avenue,' in particular, is remarkable for a neat display of Tuscan or Italian Suburban Villas.... *Fig.* 44 [the sketch mentioned], without being a precise copy of any one of these buildings, may be taken as a pretty accurate representation of their general appearance." The villa photographed is larger and has more architectonic elaboration in the Renaissance mode than that in the Downing sketch.

PLATE 42.   Bridgeport, Conn. Bridgeport was the home town of P. T. Barnum, proponent of tinseled grandeur under the big top and proprietor of a repository of not-always authentic anomalies. Barnum's success indicates the Victorian propensity for identifying with Alice visiting Wonderland. In this old stereoscopic view the setting presents a Never-Never Land foreground of wedding-cake posts and gingerbread gateway leading to the pretentious portico-porch, the upper supports of which have not only composite-order capitals but imposts and bracketed architrave, and other brackets projecting forward under the pediment. The assembled inhabitants, in costumes denoting their calling or social status, assume stereotyped poses in a tableau that was natural and meaningful to their generation.

PLATE 43.   New Haven, Conn. This Hillhouse Avenue villa resembles the other (Plate 41) in size and shape. The complexity of its forms indicates it to be later. A horizontal band divides the walls at the level of the second-story window sills. Arches interlay the supports in portico and hooded windows. An elaborate bay window surmounts the portico and in turn forms a balcony for a recessed loggia in the attic story, the last crowned by a curved pediment. Equivalents to simple frieze windows in the earlier building here are gabled half-dormers. The new bristling effect is gained at the loss of quiet grandeur, proper to its predecessor.

PLATE 44. Hamilton, N.Y. A third-quarter-of-the-nineteenth-century dwelling recycled into a third-quarter-of-the-twentieth-century village office is an approved preservation procedure. The original features have been retained with the exception of the porch supports. These have been exchanged for practically invisible lattices, that appear to let the roof float unsupported. Slender iron posts at the corners and flanking the entrance bay do carry the load; but their structural accommodation does not compensate for their style, scale and propriety shortcomings.

PLATE 45. Schoharie, N.Y. The creative urge of the late Victorian period was expressed more in the range of the microscope than the telescope. The overall concept of this design is stilted and static, whereas there are many delightful surprises in the details. Circular motifs in the railing are repeated in the bottom panels of the doors. In addition to the odd cylindrical brackets over the posts, there are smaller, alternating dentils and modillions between them. The highly styled bulky brackets to the main cornice are strangely combined in pairs on a pendant element, with grilled panels between, over which are smaller brackets, the last adapted to the raking of the center gable. Boldly modeled ornaments concentrated at the top overburden the facade.

PLATES 46–47.   Central Village, Conn. The inchworm bracketed hoods over the second-story side windows repeat in curves the angular motif of the house cornice, whereas that in the center of the facade holds to straight lines, becoming a miniature of the larger projection above. The Palladian-type openings on the flanks are superimposed over polygonal bay windows, giving a

pagoda effect. Like the arched porch, deep eaves, belvedere crowning the broad hip roof, and quoins at the corners, the balustrade fence is Italian Renaissance. Note the ribbed stone obelisks serving as posts to either side of the front walk.

PLATE 48.   Poughkeepsie, N.Y. Captain John H. Brinkerhoff, owner of the fleet Hudson River steamer, Mary Powell (launched 1861), had steamboat elements incorporated in his home built on Hamilton Street during the 1880s. Included were undulating encircling decks, with paddle-wheel motifs in the lower railing, and an open balustraded captain's bridge above. Originally the house had another balustrade over the main cornice around the flat roof and a pilothouse with bonnet roof atop the central tower, creating a more impressive and picturesque residence. (See p. viii.)

PLATE 49.   Poughkeepsie, N.Y. This neighboring house is as beholden to traditional dry-land architecture in the Hudson River Valley as the Brinkerhoff house to the floating palace. The symmetrical five-bayed facade is an eighteenth-century form brought up to date by late nineteenth-century bracketed dress, including the third-story window motif (formerly a pediment) centered above the entrance. The square tower on the left flank is modeled after the flared-roof "pagoda" added to Washington Irving's Sunnyside in 1847, though it does not compose as attractively with the rest of the building as in Irving's "elegant little snuggery."

PLATE 50. Lewiston, Me. The French Mansard style in America flourished after additions were made to the Louvre in Paris during the third quarter of the nineteenth century, when the architects Visconti and Lefuel erected the Place Louis Napoleon and the west wings on the site of the extremities of the old Tuileries Palace. These constructions were in the manner of the Baroque of the early seventeenth century, rather than the later, quieter Classic. The American version was provincial, characterized by manipulation and clutter of architectural members, glaring inconsistencies in scale, and meaningless addenda. The Maine house illustrated may have been inspired by the frontispiece in G. B. Croff's *Progressive American Architecture* (1875), a perspective sketch of an "Elegant Villa" constructed after plans by the author for a client in Burlington, Vermont.

PLATE 51. St. Stephen, New Brunswick. The triple projections that characterize so many Canadian Victorian homes (Plates 16, 17, 20 and 21) here appear in a French Mansard version. The ethnic background of early Canadian settlers would have engendered an affinity for the style. As in the preceding example the house shown is executed in wood. The care required for upkeep of the intricate details is symbolized by the workmen clinging to the upper ledges. A fine Eastlake wrought-iron cresting enhances the summit of the roof.

PLATE 52. Cambridge, N.Y. In shape and size this little Hudson River region house may be compared to that at Granville Ferry, Nova Scotia (Plate 18). Both have a central pavilion flanked by porches to the first story. The spans of these porches are broad and bisected by a pendant. The sharp distinction between them stems from the Gothic styling of the Canadian dwelling as opposed to the bracketed mode of the American. In the first, forms droop downward and the house sinks into the ground. The second is buoyed up on a respectable basement, and walls rise to hovering eaves, with no roof slope visible. The Eastlake cutout pattern carries across the podium oblivious of upright supports.

PLATE 53.   Brookfield, Mass. Rusticated piers in the porch matching quoins at the corners of the pavilions, variegated wall treatment (smooth and clapboarded), and the subtle use of arches are design assets to the facade shown. Early Georgian features are used with a measure of authentic delicacy in the upper region: meander dentils and modillions support the main cornice; upturned consoles buttress the dormer windows; and blind arches articulate the square chimneys. The dull proportions of the wide porch spoil the good effect the house otherwise would have had.

PLATE 54.   Coastal Me. This flush-board house has a restrained simulated rustication. The first story is preceded by an airy and relatively plain porch. Lavishness of design has been concentrated at the top. The curved gambrel gable and pedimented dormers breaking the dipping mansard roof have windows enframed by colonnettes, spandrels and bracketed hoods; and there are cornices and finials at the crest of the roof. Hood molds over the second-story fenestration are meager. The oversized brackets supporting the abbreviated horizontal cornice elongated into the area under the gable are architecturally illogical.

PLATE 55. Bangor, Me. Comparing this house to the three just considered makes one realize that the wide American porch seldom enhances a house and the smaller entrance shelter generally is more attractive. The slightly curved or low-pitched hoods over the windows set a cadence that climaxes in the dramatic upsurge of the cornice over the entrance bay. The good sense of scale between parts creates a composition enjoyable to the eye.

PLATE 56. View of Augusta, Me. (M. F. Sweetser, *Picturesque Maine*, Portland, 1880, facing p. 26). The Kennebec River flows through Maine's capital city, and its administrative buildings are on the west side. This photograph of the late 1870s was taken from the top of the State House, designed by Charles Bulfinch and built 1829-32. (It was to be enlarged in 1911). In the foreground is the Executive Mansion, originally in the Classic Revival manner of the early 1830s, remodeled and added to in the villa style after 1852 for James G. Blain. Here he received news of becoming Maine's only nominee for President. State Street runs northward past the front of the old Augusta House, in the upper left corner of the photograph. The original structure was built in 1832; the later addition has a mansard roof and forest of chimneys.

PLATE 57. View of Portland, Me. (M. F. Sweetser, *Picturesque Maine*, Portland, 1880, facing p. 14). Settled in the seventeenth century and called Falmouth until given its present name in 1786, Portland has undergone dire vicissitudes. It has been methodically destroyed once in each century up to the twentieth: by an Indian raid in 1675, by British bombardment in 1775, and by fire in 1866. The panorama shows Maine's largest city twenty years after the last catastrophe, at which time its population was 40,000. Overlooking the collection of gambrel-roofed and bracketed houses and the reservoir to the right, in the distance may be seen the water that surrounds the almost-island site.

PLATE 58. Charlestown, N.H. (*Views of Charlestown, N. H.,* Brattleboro, Vt., n. d.). View of Sherman Parris' garden at the end of the nineteenth century: the vista is down the main path, bordered with flowers and dotted with lamps for night illumination. Greenhouses on the right are centered on the fanciful square summerhouse on the left, with an assortment of dependencies grouped at its rear. Towers, cupolas, and mansard roofs with dormers lend charm to the service buildings.

PLATE 59.   View of Leominster, Mass. *(Leominster Illustrated,* 2nd ed., n. d., Gardner, Mass., plate 2). This late nineteenth-century camera impression was made from the tower of the Unitarian Church, one of several handsome religious buildings facing the town common, whose other landmarks included the Civil War Soldiers' Monument and the depot of the Old Colony Railroad. The street seen in the distance is Grove Avenue. Most of the houses are variations of a compact scheme and look as though they were put up by the same contractor. Construction was recent, and landscaping had not yet been developed.

PLATES 60-61. Hartford, Conn. (Plate 60, photo by R. S. de Lameter, *Sunlight Pictures — Hartford,* Hartford, 1892, and Plate 61, *Hartford Illustrated,* Brooklyn, N.Y., 1899). In 1836 Samuel Colt secured a patent on the first practical revolving firearm and started a factory in Patterson, New Jersey. It failed in 1842. Colt lost his patent rights and turned to submarines. Receiving an order from the federal government for 1,000 pistols at the outbreak of the Mexican War in 1846, Colt regained his patents and opened a new firearm plant in Connecticut, first at Whitneyville and later at his birthplace, Hartford.

He prospered, and in 1857-58 he built a home on Wethersfield Avenue. It was called Armsmear and combined medieval, Italian and Oriental elements. The pointed arches and trellis bulbous dome on the round corner pavilion and tracery greenhouse on the left flank are somewhat Gothic, somewhat Sara-cenic. The tall square corner tower with projecting balcony and bracketed eaves recalls the turrets of the 300-foot-long exotic New Haven Railroad Station, designed and built by Henry Austin in 1848, since razed. Austin planned many residences, and probability credits him with Armsmear.

PLATE 62.   Lee, Mass. (J. Copeland & Co., *Streets, Public Buildings and General Views of Lee, Mass.*, Pittsfield, Mass., 1886). The relationship of the main block of the Wellington Smith house to its tower and grouping of dependencies and the size and character of its elements may be compared to those in the Griffin Place residence in Woburn (Plate 66). The house here in Lee has considerable more grace in its concave hips and gables, curvilinear dormer enframements, complex roof over the portico, and iron cresting along the porch cornice. Note the sculpture in the yard.

PLATE 63. Woburn, Mass. (Board of Trade, *Woburn — An Historical and Descriptive Sketch of the Town,* Woburn, 1885). The residence of Charles B. Bryant on Montvale Avenue evidently was planned by the builder of the Cummings house (Plate 79). One finds in both the identical fenestration, porch, bracket details, and even the same front gable — not so much in evidence in this view because on the profile of the building to the left. The cupolas constitute the chief difference between them, the other having paired windows in each side. The formal garden in the foreground is not very exciting, but in Woburn it must have made the Bryant estate something of a showplace.

PLATE 64. Woburn, Mass. (Board of Trade, *Woburn — An Historical and Descriptive Sketch of the Town,* Woburn, 1885). The coupled semicircular-arched windows in the second story and peculiar polygonal-headed dormers are practically identical to those in the Bryant and Cummings residences (Plates 63 and 79). This, the J. Q. A. Brackett house on Highland Street, shows more stress laid on detailing of members (in porches, bay windows, entablature and quoins) and less (actually none) on roof sweep. The front shown would be in perfect balance were it not for the bay window being pushed to one side of the projecting pavilion.

PLATE 65.   Woburn, Mass. (Board of Trade, *Woburn — An Historical and Descriptive Sketch of the Town,* Woburn, 1885). The informal scheme of the Hon. John Cummings house on Bedford Street does not preclude elegance. Elegance is achieved through use of classic motifs, including one triangular pediment as a window hood. The portico, with its composite-order columns set on pedestals, is supplemented by an arcuated porch to one side, balanced by a bay window on the other. All three have balustrades above on the same level. The house has plain walls but an elaborate roof form, including a variety of dormer windows. The ladies on the portico awaiting their equipage indicate scale.

PLATE 66. Woburn, Mass. (Board of Trade, *Woburn — An Historical and Descriptive Sketch of the Town,* Woburn, 1885). The tight, cluttered aspect of Victorian architecture is nowhere better displayed in a medium-sized house than in that of Griffin Place, whose grounds similarly were crowded with de- pendencies. The saving grace is simplicity in massing, to which details are subservient. The fence encloses the property appropriately. In this and the preceding photograph, taken in the early eighties, we can see that the Mauve Decade had not yet overshadowed every structure in America.

PLATE 67. West Brookfield, Mass. The shorn look in the lower part of this residence suggests the deletion of a first-story porch, which act was accompanied by the planting of trimmed evergreens in aligned modern nursery-man's style. At least some attempt has been made to tie in the abbreviated shelter left over the entrance with the style of the building. A polychrome slate pattern overspreads the roof, and a bit of ironwork still caps the tower.

PLATE 68. Bangor, Me. The reserve of the little mansard-roofed cottage above harkens back to the period of the pure revivals. Ionic portico columns and plain pilasters at the corners of the building are set on pedestals and support an encircling entablature. Windows are enframed by a plain molding and have a frieze and cornice hood mold over them. Dormers have curved or triangular pediments and are flanked by console buttresses. The roof form suggests a mastaba tomb, which Egyptian association is furthered by the pylon profile of the gate posts.

PLATE 69.   Cold Spring, N.Y. Situated on a slope draining toward the front adds height to the facade of the cottage, and it gives cause for the conspicuous stairway rising to the ornate porch. The walls are of brick up to the first-story cornice, and there are drip molds over the segmented arched windows. A mansard roof scoops upward from the bracketed cornice except over the entrance, where upright walls form a square tower, whose summit resembles a Tibetan chorten.

PLATE 70.   Milford, Mass. In this compact little dwelling with the coziness of an old sampler, the builder has devoted time and thought to achieving interesting details. The appeal of his results is much dependent upon the size of the building. The dormer combination on a large house would look inharmonious yet here accrues quaint acceptance. The tiny portico cushioned between the bay windows makes a comfortable-looking entrance. Perhaps the worst of the original features was stretching the parts of the portico to make the expanded side porch. Modern alterations have made it a disaster area by substituting toothpick trellises for the proper wooden posts.

PLATE 71. Grafton, Mass. The box dormer, usually the ugliest of traditional architectural forms, in this instance is the crowning achievement of the facade. Its extremities follow the angles of the mansard, and the "curtained" inner edge suggests a procenium arch. One cannot say that the front porch makes a dramatic entrance, but it accords with the character of the house. One assumes the door and windows to have been stripped of some sort of more sympathetic trim.

PLATE 72. Woburn, Mass. (Board of Trade, *Woburn — An Historical and Descriptive Sketch of the Town,* Woburn, 1885). Stephen Dow's villa on Myrtle Street is Italian Renaissance up to the main cornice, above which it becomes French Second Empire. Rusticated walls, cornice hoods over the windows, an arched entrance portico with balustrade railing above, and brackets to the deep eaves all are of Latin origin, whereas the mansard roof is a Gallic covering. The Latin takes top prize, inasmuch as the chimney shapes and belvedere (barely visible in the photograph) are Italian.

PLATE 73. Schoharie, N.Y. The full two-storied three-bayed house descended from the early New England "half house," and it attained its most widespread patronage in the city as the row house. It persevered as a good minimum detached residence as long as traditional architecture lasted. It was prone to acquiring excrescences for added accommodations as needed. The introduction of the mansard roof provided them at the top. With proper elaboration to the front porch the owner could feel that he was keeping abreast of the Victorian Joneses.

PLATE 74. New Berlin, N.Y. This example started with basically the same scheme as that in Plate 73. A room has been appended to its right flank, and a tower and polygonal pavilion beyond have been added to its left side. The porch is extended around the front corner leading to the secondary entrance in the tower. The result looks like a structure that could not decide whether it was to be a town house or a country house. The matter is settled by the setting.

PLATE 75.   Hyde Park, N.Y. The bay window looks very well on the side of this house, but the builder was not content to leave well enough alone. He repeated it at the opposite front corner, swung the main house cornice as an extra bonus around the top, capped it by a belvedere made up of a sequence of dormers, each with its hood cornice, and, for good measure, ran the mansard coping cornice and iron cresting around the summit. The Eastlake designs in the crestings of both buildings on this full-page spread are noteworthy. Otherwise the only appealing feature here is the arched roof on bracketed posts that juts forward over the front steps.

PLATE 76. Leicester, Mass. In this facade, duller than a checkerboard, even arches at the entrance and in the third story fail to bring life to its monotonous layout. The three pavilions are of about the same width; they are cut horizontally by cornices into three nearly equal levels. The design would have been a little better if the porch cornice had not continued across the center pavilion, and at least one form had been allowed to dominate. The roof does not fit the eaves overhang. The three sets of steps side by side, to the main entrance and two side porches, are awkward but therefore consistent with everything else about the composition.

PLATE 77.   Sherburne, N.Y. The break in the ogee curve of the mansard roof ties in with the jog in the porch arches and angles in the hood molds over the windows and tops of the dormers. Six-paned sashes in the windows of the main part of the house indicate its having been built around the middle of the nineteenth century, whereas the narrower single-paned sashes in the wing are later. Except for the placing of the iron cresting precariously on the outer edge of the crown mold, the porch is a credit to the practice of Eclectic architecture.

PLATE 78.   Milford, Mass. The dip of the cupola roof is repeated in the mansard and in the front gable. On a smaller scale it appears in the bracketed hood over the arched window in the center of the second story, in the hood molds over the lower windows, and as heads of the lights in the front doors.

The half-round arch in the porch figures in the windows on axis — including in the lantern — and in the dormers to either side of the gable. Only the finical outline of the dormers remains unrelated to any other element.

PLATE 79.   Woburn, Mass. (Board of Trade, *Woburn — An Historical and Descriptive Sketch of the Town,* Woburn, 1885). The residence of Eustace Cummings, Esq., on East Street, has been compared to the Bryant house in the same town (Plate 63). The Cummings house is slightly more pretentious, having two bay windows in the first story and quoins at the corners that are not present in the other. It sits on a more pronounced terrace, the undulation of which reflects the upsurge of the roof and therefore makes a suitable base for the building.

PLATE 80. Cape May, N.J. Frivolous finery goes with seasonal vacation houses by the sea. The principle was established firmly at Brighton, England, with the construction of the Mughal-style Royal Pavilion during the regency of George IV. Even before the American Revolution Cape May had become a seashore resort, and afterwards it was the favorite watering place for Philadelphians. During the mid-nineteenth century it went by the name of Cape Island. This later cottage has minuscule composite capitals to the porch colonnade. The cutout work on its gables is more in evidence.

PLATE 81.   Bridgton, Me. After one has stripped off all the late nineteenth-century dress from this Maine farmhouse — including brackets, bay windows and cupola, partial gables and jerkin-headed roofs, partial dormers and summerhouse addendum to the porch — one finds that the basic elements are traditional, eighteenth-century New England. They include plan and form.

There is a transverse center hall with two rooms on either side, the fireplaces and chimneys between each pair. The house proper is covered by a hip-on-gable roof, a gambrel variation. The ell extends sidewise and develops into the attached barn and service building.

PLATE 82. Spencer, Mass. This, the preceding and the following examples indicate how popular the gazebo or open octagonal pavilion was at the elbow of porches in the late Victorian period. The plan of this house is as conservative as that of the Maine farmhouse; and if Downing — or somebody else — had not popularized the American verandah and use of brackets, and the mansard roof had remained obscure, the residence of the end of the nineteenth century would have been indistinguishable from that of a century earlier.

PLATE 83.   Catskill, N.Y. Shades of the Alhambra overcast the tight little arches of the porch. The upper part of the awkward spaces between the clustered colonnettes should be and may have been bridged by some sort of latticework. Neither the condition nor motif needed would have been derived from the famous Moorish palace. The grilles under the short end of the porch seem to have been replaced incorrectly. Squeezing together of elements, such as the roof-hood over the center window in the second story, cornice that pushes up in front of the parapet railing, and slightly elevated dormer, is what makes some Victorian architecture sadly laughable.

PLATE 84. Seneca Falls, N.Y. To raise one side of a formally balanced house a full story and superimpose virtually the identical roof form on the two levels seems a rather naive way to achieve an asymmetrical, picturesque composition. The same methodical way of thinking would account for the insertion of the arch unit from the lower porch in the recess over the doorway. Paired windows are repeated monotonously. The house is like a song of recurring refrains but without much in the way of verses in between.

PLATE 85.   Seneca Falls, N.Y. Like a miniature residence is this carriage house of masonry in cubic form. Rich-textured effects are achieved in the upper portion of the walls through assorted ways of laying bricks. Vertical edges of the building and heads and sills of openings are picked out in con-trasting white limestone. The entrance bay, dormers and cupola are covered by "Queen Anne" gables, whose delicacy introduces a feminine note in an otherwise masculine design.

PLATE 86. New Haven, Conn. Perhaps it was striving after richness of effect that made late Victorian designers brush over the matter of keeping architectural forms distinct. Here the portico is a hospitable and dignified shelter, of coupled columns on pedestals and supporting a horizontal entablature; but its structure and function are confused by the attached lounging verandah, with five front arches in three sizes. A tower by nature is an upright form, yet here its verticality is obscured through being divided by the front edge of the second-story cornice. The pavilion at the far corner is stifled by the two-story bay window and the gable superimposed on the mansard roof. Fancy is best expressed architecturally in ornament, but forms should be left to logic.

PLATE 87. Watkins Glen, N.Y. The tightly corseted Victorian lady, with flaring hoop or bulging bustle, was the fashion counterpart to contemporary architectonic distortion. The cavernous portal and ample arcaded piazza hardly accord with the heavy walls pierced by narrow fenestration of the building they precede. The main tower is cast into a stylized anthropomorphic being, and the polygon at the right has a roof faceted like a gargantuan gem. Time and the weather have contributed to the ghostly effect.

PLATE 88.   Brookfield, Mass. The square New England house was so logical, its rooms grouped around first one and then two chimneys (the latter to
allow for a center hall) and covered by a steeply pitched roof, its use became
traditional. In time, repetition created monotony and fostered the search for
variety. The easy solution was adding extra features, whereby a new look was
achieved without altering the basic scheme. The solution created problems, as
here, where protruding bays catch the wind and bring cold air into rooms, re-
quiring storm windows; and old-style gabled roofs empty onto flat projections,
necessitating special leaders at the front to carry away rainwater.

PLATE 89. Ridgefield, Conn. (William W. Woolett, *Old Homes Made New*, New York, 1879). The "Queen Anne" style from England was just getting under full steam in America when J. Howard King, of Albany, had his old gambrel-roofed summer house in Ridgefield brought up to date in the manner shown. Picturesque tower, bay window, chimney stacks, and porch and gable elaboration were the modernizing elements; and the old post-and-rail fence became post-and-spike. The jardiniere already was on the premises and acquired planting. Note the slate patterns on the tepee-shaped roof of the tower.

PLATE 90.   Earlville, N.Y. An interesting and pleasing combination of forms are the slender turret with bonnet embraced by broad gabled pavilions at right angles, the elements linked at the base by a frilly entrance porch. The open timberwork under raking eaves is graceful, and the square-and-octagon pattern of slates in two colors on the tower roof is engaging. With hood molds over the rectangular windows, the plainness of the corbel-arched openings seems wanting.

PLATE 91. Lowell, Mass. Except for remote affinities to the chalet, this Massachusetts house owes little to historic modes. Referred to as the "Stick Style," the main characteristic is structural timbers semi-exposed. Ornaments are pierced and cut out of wood, concentrated beneath gable and cornice overhangs, in the porch, and under windows. Unusual importance is given the roof, not only the coverings of house proper and tower, but including those of the porte-cochère and portico, and sheds over the first-story windows. White paint on the walls, like the planting, is inappropriate modern innovation.

PLATE 92.   Lowell, Mass. The enclosed foyer coming forward the entire depth of the porch is an odd device. It serves as base for another oddity, the polygonal bay window at second-story level. More gross than odd is the dormer window at the front. At least it serves its purpose, of lighting the garret, whereas the dormers at the sides of the house are obstructed by chimneys. An openwork frieze of turnings has been removed from the street side of the porch but may be seen intact along the flank to the viewer's right.

PLATE 93.   Lunenburg, Nova Scotia. The square and polygonal forms in the top two stories of the axial projection are reversed from the order opposite. Here the center motif resembles that of the other Lunenburg house shown earlier (Plate 16), with three arches at entrance level, two above, and one in each plane of the belvedere, which is crowned by a dipping roof. This downtown Lunenburg house is quieter in design, being free from other excrescences and capped by a gently sloping hip roof. Jigsaw elaboration over openings is a subtle and proper use of ornament.

PLATE 94.   Naples, Me. Victorian buildings often are more charming in part than in their entirety. The curve of the porch sweeps around concentric to the prismatic tower, whose flaring roof and lower part of the third-story wall stand out like spinning dancers' skirts. The open spandrels of the porch arches have a carosel quality, suggested also by the crowning motifs of the tower. One's mind swings pleasantly through associations with this corner structure, but to allow one's attention to wander to the static forms beyond is to bring one's reverie to an abrupt standstill.

PLATE 95.   Ridgefield, Conn. Snow and a gray day isolate and flatten building and landscape features into a Grandma Moses composition. The house itself is prim and self-contained, and looks as though it might have been built elsewhere and left here by chance. The scene occurs too often in the United States — the existence of a house unrelated to its setting — to lead us to imagine otherwise than that the placing was intentional, though hardly planned.

PLATE 96.   Lowell, Mass. (Frank P. Hill, *Lowell Illustrated,* 1884). In the William H. Anderson residence portico and porte-cochère are combined as preface to the four-storied entrance tower forming the apex of the complex pile. The ornate weathervane is but one of many finials capping hip roofs, gables and balcony-railing posts. English "black-and-white" timbering and Dutch shingles combine on the walls. The dependencies are detached but manage to continue the structural establishment over an impressively broad tract.

PLATE 97. Providence, R.I. The panoply of late nineteenth-century styles lined up along a residential avenue may be likened to as many actors in period dress appearing for the curtain call of a pageant. Richardsonian Romanesque, French Mansard, "Queen Anne," bracketed house and Italian villa are in sequence down the block. The escape to exotic modes indicates unrest, and it created the Victorian city made up of frustration symbols.

PLATE 98. Cape May, N.J. The Stick Style of the 1870s, due to its steep roofs, oversized dormers, ungainly chimneys, shadowy porches, and weather-stained natural wood, often produces a brooding atmosphere and "gothick" mood. On a bleak winter's day such a house seems the habitation of trolls and goblins. Under such conditions the conscious striving for picturesqueness on the part of the designer has achieved its objective.

PLATE 99. Milford, Mass. *(History of Milford,* no bibliographical information available). No less Stick Style than the foregoing, the polychromy adapted to the frame-and-panel construction focuses attention on surface patterns and supposedly diminishes speculation on spectral inhabitants inside. But the dark, wet surfaces take on their own brand of unreality; and here a sophisticated witch could lodge as naturally as other supernatural beings amidst ruin and decay. With so many angles—painted or otherwise—the style provides a multiplicity of places for things to go bump in the night.

PLATE 100.   St. Johnsbury, Vt. Designed by local architect Lambert Packard and completed in 1888, the C. R. Stevens house, with its relatively low-pitched roof and unified wall treatment, suggests a relaxed atmosphere. Porches are concentrated at the front corner opposite the polygonal tower with its campaniform bonnet. Shortly before the picture was taken the spindlework on the verandah frieze was boxed in and the window shutters removed. Tiny Palladian windows pierce the gables, and "Queen Anne" chimneys soar upward from the roof.

PLATE 101.   Lowell, Mass. Yankee conservatism underlies the semblance of free and casual forms in this wood house. In spite of the difference of treatment displayed in the front pavilions flanking the portico, the house adheres basically to a formal plan. Rooms are disposed to either side of a transverse central hall. Pointed or jerkin-headed dormers, with single, double or triple windows in them, single or grouped windows below, and the porte-cochère jutting at one side are only costume accessories on a bilaterally symmetrical body.

PLATE 102. Cape May, N.J. The ideal of eclectic innovation in late nineteenth-century architecture encouraged provincial builders in erecting dispro-
portionate abortions. One can hardly imagine an assemblage of more dishar-
monious elements per cubic foot than in this corner house at Cape May. Yet
each of the elements would be acceptable in appropriate context. The roof
resembles a nightmare in cubist style.

PLATE 103. Staten Island, N.Y. Unlike other Alpine chalets shown earlier (Plates 10, 11, 28 and 29) here an example is perched appropriately on a hill. The characteristic upper balcony is pulled in under the gable and reduced in size, if not in elaboration. The corner turret introduces an extraneous vertical shaft to the normally low-lying chalet form, but its topmost lookout responds romantically to the stairway up the cliff.

PLATE 104.   North Bennington, Vt. (Photo by Conrad R. Hoffman, Jr.). The residence of John G. McCullough, Governor of Vermont during 1902-04, is characterized by clapboard walls pierced by narrow round-topped windows, bracketed cornice covered by a mansard roof, an extensive porch with curved ends and a projecting porte-cochère, basement arches, balustrade, and dead-eye braces capping octagonal posts set on pedestals. The casual placing of the square belvedere superstructure gives the impression of a helmeted giant's head peering over the rooftop. The skyrocket turret at the right corner of the house looks poised for moon flight.

PLATE 105. Hartford, Conn. (Photo by R. S. de Lameter, *Sunlight Pictures — Hartford,* Hartford, 1892). The residence of William B. Clarke, at the corner of Farmington Avenue and Laurel Street, was representative of homes of the upper middle merchant class mushrooming in second-class American cities during the period of reconstruction following the Civil War. The brick house contained rooms dictated by social protocol, such as reception hall and formal parlor, more casual family rooms, including a billiard room, the dining room, kitchen and services, and bedrooms for family and domestics. Its architecture was no more or no less American than that of the Washington Monument.

PLATE 106. Amherst, Mass. (Photo by Edward P. Harris, *Sunlight Pictures — Amherst,* New York, 1881). The original, compact, mansard-roof house at the left had been enlarged by the "Queen Anne" addition at the right and was serving as home of the Theta Delta Chi fraternity of Amherst when this picture was taken. The result illustrates the difference between early eclectic features — cornices, finials and keystones, dentils and consoles, pedestals and pediments — and later Eastlake abstractions — cleancut porch posts, simple lattice railings, and plain horizontal moldings and chimney shaft. The latter was prelude to twentieth-century functionalism.

PLATE 107.   Springfield, Mass. Recovery from the financial depression of the early 1870s was marked by the construction of large and imaginative residences. Fashioned of indigenous timber, the architect has resorted more to invention than to imitation. Square, triangle and circle, pyramid, cone and slender upright, closed and open forms are combined into a mass interesting from any angle. The American verandah is greatly played up for both its livable and decorative value. Not a Classic order or Gothic window is to be found, and neither is missed.

PLATE 108.   Woburn, Mass. (Board of Trade, *Woburn — An Historical and Descriptive Sketch of the Town,* Woburn, 1885). The James Skinner house on Montvale Avenue is an ideal example of the "Queen Anne" style. It stresses features derived from the Middle Ages: the steep roof, articulated chimney stacks, exposed timber construction, including posts and struts in the porch, second-story overhangs, and a bay window over the entrance. The expanse of encircling porch is American. Window panes as large as these came into use only after the Civil War.

PLATE 109. Fitchburg, Mass. New York Architects McKim, Mead and White's "colonial tour" of New England in 1877 bore fruit in raising many colonial-manner residences on home soil during the last two decades of the century. Motifs mostly were authentic, though often combined in new, complex ways. Thus we find a fusion of bay windows and portico-porch, with balustrade above carried around all, and a grouping of appendices of various kinds at the ends. A dormer window with console buttresses on a parapet replace the usual pediment (see Plate 6). Lesser dormers are to right and left. The propriety of the dipping mansard roof is questionable.

PLATE 110.   St. Johnsbury, Vt. Hip roof with cresting at the apex, eye-brow dormer, two cone-shaped roofs, one to a cylindrical turret, and an up-stairs porch on consoles are features that attract our notice only after the bold curlicues in relief surrounding the Palladian window in the principal gable. The low pediment over the front steps also contains such embellishments but on a small scale. Attenuated urn-shaped posts and lattices are incorporated in a homely porch that extends part way around each side of the house. Overhang of second story is an honest expression of floor level, which principle figured in the Venetian Gothic style, popularized by John Ruskin's *The Seven Lamps of Architecture* (1849) and *Stones of Venice* (1851).

PLATE 111. Towanda, Penn. A personal interpretation of the "Queen Anne" style here consists of a ponderous, square brick block crowned by a hip roof, with appended features huddled in two camps at opposite extremities. At the farther front corner are two porches, first and second levels, the gabled roof of the second keying in with the dormer. On the near flank are two tall chimneys with vertical ribs, a gable and a semi-detached porte-cochère. Posts of the last are set on boulders, Japanese fashion; and in the front porches are Chinese railings. A flair for odd corner treatment shows up in the tiny angle window in the dormer and in the dropped roof and cornice level at the near edge of the building.

PLATE 112.   Concord, N.H. "East Indian exuberance" describes the architectural treatment of this residence. The plan of the principal mass is that of the *Shri-yantra,* of the square cosmic city with projecting gateways centered on the four sides. Balustrades (which originated in India and came to Europe during the Renaissance), Dravidian posts and bracket arches adorn porticos and walls above them. Brackets, of course, are from Hindustan; and openings at roof level are modeled on facade arches to *chaitya* halls. The superstructure reflects the *stupa* form and is the summit of sacred Mount Sumeru. But even lofty Brahman eloquence needs a practical American service wing at the back.

PLATE 113.   Concord, N.H. Plain and straightforward is this nearby house on whose front the sun falls flatly, and no aura of Oriental splendor illuminates its sides. Suggestions of the Swiss chalet, in stick braces to eaves and in gables, and especially in the porch on the near flank, constitute its only reference to exoticism. Whereas the house opposite may be compared to a potentate's palace, the forest of aerials on the roof and outside stairs on the service ell testify to this example's serving as a multiple-family dwelling — the modern equivalent to the Victorian boarding house.

PLATE 114. Bradford, Vt. There are two movements of forms in this appealing little structure. One is horizontal; and it consists of polygons spanning the front, two bay windows linked by an arched porch. The other is vertical; and it is composed of two steeply pitched gables connected below by the undulating elements described, especially by the broad pediment over the entrance bay, and above by the front plane of the crosswise roof. Ornaments are minimal and carpenter's gothic.

PLATE 115. Hudson vicinity, N.Y. Frederick E. Church amassed a fortune through sales of his large canvases of rugged landscapes. Quest of the exotic took him to Syria and Palestine, and besides his own paintings he brought back crates of art objects collected for his proposed Oriental villa on the lordly Hudson. With help from Calvert Vaux, Church devised the design for the Eastern palace erected in 1870. It was called Olana, from the Arabic, meaning "Our Place on High"; and it was a colorful assembly of Persian, Moorish, Saracenic, Chinese and Japanese elements. Here, for thirty years, Frederick Church worked prodigiously, entertained lavishly, and lived in the grand style. In the mid 1960s his heirs decided to dispose of the 327-acre estate. Thanks to an illustrated article in *Life* magazine, a sum of $310,000 was raised and Olana became a museum and park. As such it has become one of the most famous Victorian houses in America, and thus its inclusion as the final specimen in this *Treasury of Lesser-Known Examples* is quite illicit.

INDEX

(References are to plate numbers.)